THE
MILKMAN

Tom Phelps

SHIRE PUBLICATIONS

Published in Great Britain in 2010 by Shire Publications
Ltd, Midland House, West Way, Botley, Oxford OX2 0PH,
United Kingdom.
44-02 23rd St, Suite 219, Long Island City, NY 11101
E-mail: shire@shirebooks.co.uk   www.shirebooks.co.uk

A CIP catalogue record for this book is available from the
British Library.

Shire Library no. 603   •   ISBN-13: 978 0 74780 801 5

Tom Phelps has asserted his right under the Copyright,
Designs and Patents Act, 1988, to be identified as the
author of this book.

Designed by Tony Truscott Designs, Sussex, UK
and typeset in Perpetua and Gill Sans.
Printed in China through Worldprint Ltd.

10 11 12 13 14   10 9 8 7 6 5 4 3 2 1

COVER IMAGE
This depiction of the typically cheerful milkman appeared
im March 1937 on the front cover of the *United Dairies
Magazine and Price List*, issued free to the milkman's
customers. It contained recipes, household tips, children's
stories and film reviews.

TITLE PAGE IMAGE
This milkman is hard at work in the centennial year of
Express Dairies, in 1964.

CONTENTS PAGE IMAGE
The new 'pintie' bottle, like its predecessor, was used by
dairies to advertise. This brought in additional revenue,
and the products it publicised, such as breakfast cereals,
had the added bonus of increasing milk sales.

DEDICATION
This book is dedicated to my sister, Mary Elizabeth Phelps,
who passed away in December 2009.

ACKNOWLEDGEMENTS
I am grateful for the assistance of the following people:
John Deadman, Steve Edwards (Whitehouse Dairy), Neil
Garner, Paul Gray (Birmingham and Midlands Museum of
Transport), Paul Luke (Editor, MBN), Bob Malcolm, Dave
Marden, Chris Munn (Dairy Crest), Libby Russell
(Cotteswold Dairies), and Jane Widdowson (Kirby and
West Dairies).

Photographs are acknowledged as follows:

Dairy Crest, pages 58, 62 (top), and 63 (bottom);
J. Deadman, pages 48 (bottom), and 52; Getty Images,
page 34 (bottom); Kirby & West, page 10; Paul Luke,
pages 3, 14 (top), 32, 39 (top), 53, and 61 (top); Bob
Malcolm, pages 8, 20, 27 (bottom), and 36 (middle);
D. & P. M. Sheldon, pages 56 (top) and 63 (top); Andy
Solloway, page 62 (bottom); Roger Workman, Cotteswold
Dairies, pages 13 (bottom left), and 56 (bottom).

Shire Publications is supporting the Woodland Trust, the UK's leading woodland conservation charity, by funding the dedication of trees.

CONTENTS

THE EARLY MILKMAN: BEFORE 1900

IN 1643 the Lord Mayor of London, Isaac Pennington, issued an ordnance forbidding the calling or sale of milk before 8 o'clock in the morning on Mondays to Saturdays, and on Sundays before 9 o'clock. The milkmen shouted their wares and their route was known as a 'walk'. The dairy business did not develop until the mid-seventeenth century, when the need for mass-produced milk grew as towns expanded. Before then, villagers obtained all the milk, cheese and butter they required from their own cattle. In the eighteenth century, when Sheffield was still a small town, Francis Chantrey, who was to become one of Britain's most famous sculptors, could be seen on the road from Norton, working as a milk boy with a donkey and a barrel of milk. Milk was sold by milkmen, and sometimes milkwomen, who carried two pails supported by a yoke fitting on their shoulders. They were dirty, uncouth individuals, and the women, or 'milk kitties', were not always the pretty maids portrayed in pictures.

If the milkmen were of dubious character, then the product they sold was even more so. These unscrupulous people would add as much water as they could to the milk. Thomas Baird wrote in 1794:

> Retail milk dealers are for the most part the refuse of other employments, possessing neither character, decency, manners nor cleanliness. No delicate person could possibly drink the milk, were they fully acquainted with the filthy habits of these dealers.

He considered that the profit margin was so good that they should not be tempted to adulterate the milk, but they did so not only with water but with 'other worse mixtures'. Certainly it was common practice to use water from the horse trough.

These yoke-and-pail milkmen had not improved in character by the time Queen Victoria came to the throne. Charles Dickens gave an insight into the conduct of a fictitious Victorian milkman in *David Copperfield* (1849):

Opposite: Charlie Andrews, who weighed over 18 stone, worked for R. Higgs & Sons from 1869.

An eighteenth-century milkmaid with her yoke and pails. This method of carrying milk was used in Britain for over 250 years. In truth, rather than a pretty girl, the job was more likely to be done by an uncouth individual with poor personal hygiene.

This yoke was used by milkmen who worked for R. Higgs & Son. Richard Higgs started milk rounds in the 1850s but his father, Caleb, had farmed in Walworth from 1820.

The milkman, after shaking his head at her darkly, released her chin, and with anything rather than good-will opened his can, and deposited the usual quantity in the family jug. This done, he went away, muttering, and uttered the cry of his trade next door, in a vindictive shriek.

This treatment of the servant girl was because Micawber had failed to pay his bill.

When the magazine *Punch* was first published in 1852, it began a long campaign to achieve supplies of pure milk. Herbert Asquith, Liberal Prime Minister from 1908 to 1916, recalled in a

A Victorian canvassing card used by the milkmen who worked for Welford's.

AWARDED 21 GOLD AND SILVER MEDALS FOR PURITY AND EXCELLENCE.

PURE NEW MILK
of richest quality, from our protected Farms,
4d. per Quart.

NURSERY MILK.
Produced on our own Farms at Harlesden and Willesden from specially-fed and selected Cows.
5d. per Quart.

Asses' Milk (Specialité for Invalids) per qt.
Goats' ,, ,, ,, per qt.

MILK PREPARATIONS.

	Per Champagne Bottle. Large.	Small.
FACSIMILE HUMAN MILK ...	1/0	0/7
Peptonized Milk	1/0	0/7
Specially Prepared Sweet Whey	1/0	0/7
Butter Milk	0/6	0/4
Koumiss	1/2	0/8
Sterilized Milk for Shipboard ...	0/9	0/6

CREAM.
Best Single ... ... per qt.
Best Double ... ... per qt.
Best Double Cream and Devonshire Clotted Cream in Jugs, 7d. and 1/1 each.

BUTTER. *Per lb.*
Finest Creamery, Fresh-churned daily
Best Fresh Butter ... ...
Finest Dorset (slightly Salted) ...
Cooking Butter ... ...

EGGS. *Per doz.*
Best New Laid (Brahma) ... ...
Best Breakfast (Fresh from the Farms)
Good Cooking Eggs ... ...

CREAM CHEESE, Fresh made Daily.
Awarded 1st Prize, British Dairy Farmers' Assoc.
6d. and 1/- each.

Pure British Honey, 1/- per Jar.

From

Please supply

Date

Messrs. Welford & Sons, Ltd.

Chief Dairy and Office:

Elgin Avenue,

Maida Vale, W.

The address only to be written on this side.

POST CARD.

AFFIX HALFPENNY STAMP.

PRICE LIST.

TELEGRAMS, WELFORDS, LONDON.
TELEPHONE NO.: 7107.

WELFORD & SONS
LIMITED.

THE LARGEST DAIRY
In London.

CHIEF DAIRY AND OFFICES,
Elgin Avenue, Maida Vale, W.

BRANCH DAIRIES.

BAYSWATER.	HAMPSTEAD.
BISHOPSGATE.	HARLESDEN.
BLOOMSBURY.	HIGHGATE HILL.
BRONDESBURY.	HOLLOWAY.
BRYANSTON SQUARE.	KENSINGTON HIGH ST.
CAMDEN TOWN.	SOUTH KENSINGTON.
CHELSEA.	MAIDA VALE.
CITY.	MAIDA HILL.
COLLEGE PARK.	MAYFAIR.
FULHAM.	OXFORD STREET.

DAIRY FARMS,
HARLESDEN AND WILLESDEN, MIDDLESEX.

EMPLOYES' MODEL DWELLINGS,
1, 2, 3 BLOCKS, SHIRLAND ROAD, W.

UTENSIL DEPARTMENT,
GATEWAY HOUSE, SHIRLAND ROAD, W.

letter that many years earlier a little girl who was unwell was given a glass of milk and asked wistfully 'May I drink to the bottom?' – fearing it might be contaminated. Milkmen were referred to as carriers (and some may see irony in the medical usage of the word). The yoke was made of wood and priced in a dairy catalogue of 1880 at 12s, plus 8s for the accompanying straps. The load was extremely heavy, with two pails each containing 40 or 50 quarts of milk, as well as customers' empty cans.

A MILKMAN DELIVERS — WILLIAM FRYER

William Fryer was born in 1843 and at the age of eight was working on his father's farm at Ringmer, near Lewes, Sussex. He then worked for his brother, a dairyman, carrying yoke and pails, and when twelve he worked for a dairyman in Tunbridge Wells. In 1863 he joined Mr Painter at Lorrimore Road, Walworth, London. He had to be up at 3 a.m. to milk ten cows before the first round; then, after a quick breakfast, he would feed the cows and then go out for the second delivery. After that there would be duties such as storing hay and straw, and at night-time, after feeding the cows again, he would wash and clean all the utensils including the pails carried on his yoke. Twice a week he was required to load

grain, getting home at midnight, and he still had to be up the next morning before 4 a.m.

After two years he opened his own successful dairy at Avenue Road, Camberwell, but at the age of twenty-five he emigrated to America and started farming at Crutchfield, Massachusetts. After five years he became a stonemason at Franklin Central, New York. In 1874 he returned to England and commenced work as a milkman for R. Higgs & Sons, who were still using yokes and pails.

He served as a milkman for the next forty-two years and then took on light duties in the warehouse. He recalled that in 1861 there was a terrible epidemic of rinderpest that killed cattle and was similar to cholera in human beings. The effect on dairymen was so great that many committed suicide. He also recalled that when milk arrived by train it was warm and he had to take it back quickly to cool it ready for delivery. Hours were so long that milkmen almost fell asleep whilst working, and the Food Adulteration Act in 1870 was implemented because of the unscrupulous activities of some milkmen. He retired at seventy-nine, after seventy years of arduous work, mostly as a milkman.

William Fryer with his yoke and pail, while working for R. Higgs & Son.

George Barham, who had employed milkmen at Nell Gwynne Dairy, later founded Express Dairy in 1864, when he brought the first milk to London by train from Penshurst, Kent. Until that time most milkmen worked for themselves or for the owner of a small number of rounds. From the mid-nineteenth century the yoke and pail began to be replaced by small handcarts, each holding a large churn. The milkman was required to measure the customers' requirements into small cans.

Left: George Barham founded the Express Dairy in 1864. Milk was transported by express trains and the company's first trademark recognised the importance of the fast locomotive.

Below: A Victorian advertisement for measures and hand cans. They are 'far superior to those chopped at by machines and put together by boys'.

Eventually there was a change in attitude by milk retailers, and churns and utensils were rigorously cleansed after use at the end of the day. There also developed a determination to ensure that milk supplies would get through despite any calamities. For instance, a great snowstorm swept across southern England on 18 January 1881, with snow lying 8 feet deep. William Burgess, a twenty-one-year-old milkman, returned from his round close to death but was saved by his master, Mr Puttock, and his wife, who warmed him in front of the fire.

Collecting the money was not always easy and young Mr Wright recounted that he was offered two paintings by the impoverished American artist, James McNeil Whistler, in the 1870s, but he chose to accept £5 instead. By the end of the nineteenth century town farms were disappearing and the milkman greatly improved his attitude, appearance and the quality of his milk, but even more dramatic change would occur in the twentieth century.

PUSHING THE PRAM: 1900–19

A T THE START of the twentieth century the milkman's usual means of delivery was pushing his 'pram'. This was a three-wheeled cart that held a conical milk churn, usually made of brass. This was an easier way of delivering milk than by yoke and pail, but a few milkmen still favoured the older method: in 1914 the large dairy company of Welfords took over from Prett's Dairy a round that was still done by yoke and pail. Milkmen sold unpasteurised milk from 17-gallon churns, pushed along on these ubiquitous milk prams, which mostly had 26-inch wheels and cost between £5 and £10. There was a drawer for the milkman's books and items such as eggs and cheese.

The cheapest churns were made of steel but the proudest milkmen would have a brass version. The churn had a tap at the base that often froze in sub-zero temperatures, but a borrowed kettle of hot water would usually melt the ice; otherwise the brass-handled measure had to be dipped into the neck of the churn. Hot weather also caused problems, which churn covers made of duck feathers could alleviate, or an ice chamber might be inserted into the churn. To measure out customers' requirements, the milkman carried certified measuring dips, usually ranging from a gill to a quart, and the customers' cans that he had to fill were mostly in the same quantity ranges. Distribution to the doorstep was by a hand can holding 2½ or 3 gallons. Small cans were filled from the hand can by the measure and left on the doorstep. Later visits were made to the same houses to collect the empty cans and to deliver extra milk, for which customers this time provided their own jugs.

Pushing a milk pram was difficult when tracks were muddy or had deep ruts that froze in icy conditions. If the round was some distance from the dairy, or in hilly terrain, the milkman would have a horse-drawn open cart to carry his one or two churns. These carts cost around £25 at the beginning of the Edwardian period.

The milkman would be based either at a yard at the local dairy shop, or on a farm. In large towns and cities 'town farms' had mostly disappeared before the First World War but some survived as distribution depots.

Opposite:
Pictured in Westcotes Drive, Leicester, this milkman with his pram proudly works for Kirby & West, which was formed in 1868 when Mr West and Mr Kirby merged their milk rounds.

Above: Long & Pocock was founded by Walter Long and his brother-in-law, Walter Pocock, both from Wiltshire.

The milkman worked long hours with few benefits, although customers held him in high esteem. A typical working day would begin at 4 a.m. After breakfast he would start the first round, serving about one hundred customers. He would return to have something to eat, take on another churn, then serve the same customers again for the 'pudding' round in the middle of the day. After returning to base again, he would go out to serve his customers for the third time. At the end of the day churns, carts and utensils were thoroughly cleaned and sterilised, and polish was applied to the brass churn lids and the rails of the barrow. Perhaps the milkman would finish at 7 p.m. If the milkman was farm-based, he would almost certainly milk and feed the cattle, in addition to his round. If working from a dairy shop, he would probably be on a rota to fetch the milk by horse and cart from a nearby farm or railway station late at night.

For all this, he would be paid from 20s to 25s for a seven-day week.

It was commonplace for milkmen to give potential new customers brochures extolling the virtues of their dairy.

DAIRY SUPPLY CO., LTD., London, Edinburgh, Cork and Belfast.   63

MILK PERAMBULATORS.

Number 1.

Wheels 26 inches in diameter, iron rails. To carry a 50-quart churn.

£5.

All these patterns are well made of the best well-seasoned timber, and the designs combine lightness and strength.

The prices include painting and lining out in the best style, and in any colour, except vermilion, **5s.** extra.

Writing to order, extra.

Number 2.

Wheels 26 inches in diameter, iron rails, oval name boards. To carry a 50-quart churn.

£5 5s.

Number 3.

Wheels 26 inches in diameter, brass rails and rod round name boards, removable back, drawers for books. To carry a 68-quart churn.

£9 10s.

Number 5.

Wheels 36 inches in diameter, cranked axle, can rails and hook for kettle.

£7 10s.

FOR

DELIVERY CHURNS

Suitable for use in these Perambulators

See page 62.

Number 4.

Wheels 26 inches in diameter, brass rails and rod, extra large name boards, removable back, drawer for books. Extra finish. To carry a 68-quart churn.

£10.

Above:
An 'Edward'. This was a dairy company's 'Oscar' and was awarded for exceptional service during the 1980s and 1990s.

Left: This advertisement in the 1900 Dairy Supply Company catalogue shows various designs of milk pram that could be purchased for as little as £5.

Far left: Milk prams were in use during the 1850s. Cotteswold Dairy has a model with a protective roof.

Left: A beautiful milk pram owned by Clifford's Dairies. William Clifford started the business in Hounslow in 1874 and it continued as a family-run firm until 1993.

13

A 1910 horse-drawn float and churn belonging to J. T. Edwards. These were more appropriate for delivering to customers some distance from the milkman's premises.

Wages varied according to duties and the generosity of the employer. Some paid commission, and a typical example was to pay a halfpenny on sales of over 450 quarts a week. Others paid good conduct money of 1s a week, this being withheld for bad book-keeping or smoking on the round. Holidays were virtually non-existent but Manor Farm Dairy in London was one of the pioneers of the weekday half-holiday and the yearly week's holiday.

Looking respectable was important; a clean smock was essential, and straw boaters were worn in the summer, and often bowler hats in winter. Some unscrupulous milkmen deliberately dented customers' cans or the measuring dip to give short measure. Adulteration by adding

Some milkmen carried out their deliveries on tricycles. This advertisement appears in a catalogue produced during the First World War.

Pictured in 1908, these boys worked for Harrison's Waverley Creamery delivering milk in the Liverpool area before going to school. They would return after school to deliver again.

water occasionally occurred, and a favourite trick was to leave the churn lid open in the rain for some divine intervention.

Competition was fierce, with up to five milkmen delivering to one street in large cities. Each would have his established round, and new competitors would follow him and canvass his customers. He therefore needed to give the very best service and be courteous and polite. Many households took advantage of cheaper milk from 'cut price' vendors, who did not have rounds but walked the streets shouting their offers. One of these was a Mr Handsley but his business did not survive the pressures of the First World War.

Milk measured from churns was called 'loose' milk and was unpasteurised, but early in the twentieth century some milkmen began selling pasteurised milk, principally for infants. In 1906, after years of planning and visits to the United States and Canada, the Lane family of Manor Farm Dairy introduced pasteurised milk in bottles, and such was its popularity that their whole business was gradually converted to the new system and delivery in cans was abandoned. In 1909 Manor Farm introduced the process of homogenising milk, whereby the cream is distributed through the whole of the milk and does not rise to the top

Co-operative societies employed many milkmen and pioneered many new methods. The Eccles Society is

These brochures were issued by Manor Farm Dairy to potential customers in the period before the First World War. Manor Farm led the way on the bottling and pasteurisation of milk.

15

A MILKMAN DELIVERS — ALFRED WILLIAM ASHWELL

Alfred Ashwell left school at the age of nine and worked on a farm until he was seventeen. At the age of eighteen he commenced work as a milkman with Mr Harding in Sydenham. His duties included doing a milk round, milking two cows, and feeding and cleaning two horses; then, after the day's work, he came back at 9 p.m. to fetch milk from the railway station. In 1877, at the age of twenty-four, he married Miss Hebekeh Hunt.

The responsibilities of a wife made him look for another situation, which he found with Wraight & Dumbrill in Croxted Road, West Dulwich, which he described as being a quiet little hamlet surrounded by fields. He sold 'Pure New Milk' at 4d a quart and 'Nursery Milk' at 5d a quart. In 1914 he was nearly sixty-two and was not eligible for military service but he still did the arduous job of a milkman. Sadly, one of his beloved sons was killed in the conflict.

Affectionately known as 'Daddy' by his customers, because of his twelve children, he worked on the same round until he was knocked over by a motor car; although he struggled to keep going, he was forced to retire at the age of seventy-four. He received a pension from his firm. 'Daddy' fondly remembered the days at the turn of the century when he arrived at work at 4 a.m. and milked eight cows before beginning the first round, which he finished about 8 a.m. After breakfast he had to cut chaff and wurzels and clean out the cowshed. Following dinner, he milked the cows and then did the afternoon round, booked in and scalded the returns. He got home about 7 p.m. but was grateful he received three days holiday a year!

'Daddy' Ashwell on his round. It is clearly one of the warmer months as he is wearing his summertime straw boater, and the churn cover is in place to keep the milk cool.

believed to have been the first to introduce milk rounds, in 1879. The St George Society in Glasgow started pasteurising milk in 1904, while in 1913 the Coventry Society became the first Co-op to bottle milk. Hull followed in 1915, then Newcastle, Plymouth and the Manchester & Salford Society, all before 1920. Co-operative societies paid a cash dividend to customers, and many households welcomed this bonus. Many societies and some other dairies operated a token system whereby tokens pre-purchased from Co-op shops or milkmen were left outside the door indicating the amount of milk required.

The First World War prompted far-reaching changes, many of which were to become permanent. The Army's requirement for men, horses and vehicles made it impossible for many companies to continue to compete. Milkmen were enlisted in the forces, and horses were commandeered. Deliveries were mostly reduced to twice daily. Dairies sought to overcome these problems by coming to arrangements whereby the milk was distributed by greatly reduced fleets of vehicles and customers were exchanged to minimise the distances travelled.

These zoning agreements soon became more formal and by the end of hostilities many new partnerships had been formed and deals made that reduced competition. Rounds became larger, using fewer vehicles and making more effective use of manpower. United Dairies came into being as companies realised it was important to unite during the conflict. The Earl of Suffolk was appointed the first chairman but was killed in France in 1917 before he could preside over a board meeting. Titus Barham was now in charge of the Express Dairy

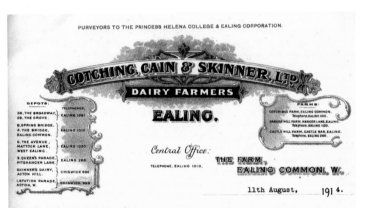

The First World War brought many problems for the milkman. Here there is a heart-felt appeal to pay the milk bill on time. Note the embellished letter-heading.

A newspaper cutting of 1917 informs customers of the milk shortage caused by war conditions.

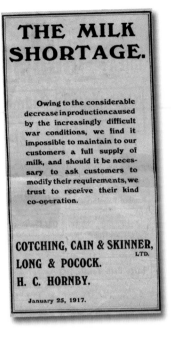

THE MILK SHORTAGE.

Owing to the considerable decrease in production caused by the increasingly difficult war conditions, we find it impossible to maintain to our customers a full supply of milk, and should it be necessary to ask customers to modify their requirements, we trust to receive their kind co-operation.

COTCHING, CAIN & SKINNER, LTD.
LONG & POCOCK.
H. C. HORNBY.

January 25, 1917.

Company, while his brother, Colonel Arthur Barham, had taken his own firm, the Dairy Supply Company, to become part of United Dairies. The First World War caused a family conflict and the two companies remained in opposition for decades, long after the brothers had died.

Other dairies remained independent, including Job's. Handel Alfred Job had worked for Louisa Roberts and her husband, and then married the widowed Louisa in 1901. By all accounts Job was a wastrel but he gave his name to a firm that was to trade for the next eight decades. Job's also had a profitable bakery business and this helped the dairy department get through the difficult wartime period.

During the First World War many dairies employed women, boys straight

One of the many women recruited during the First World War, Miss Gamble commenced work with the Alliance Dairy in January 1916. She later became a dairy shop manageress and retired in May 1959.

from school and older men in their sixties and even seventies to ensure that Britain's milk was delivered. The strain on these people was enormous. Some did two complete rounds daily. At Manor Farm, women were unable to push the large loaded prams containing bottles, but with typical ingenuity they converted their prams into donkey barrows and so were able to complete their rounds. Mrs Culver often enlisted the help of soldiers to load the churns on to her cart on wartime mornings, because the railway porters at Kingston upon Thames charged a shilling.

This young milkman carries his milk on a donkey. Many forms of transport were used until conventional milk floats became commonplace by 1930.

Milkmen throughout the twentieth century have helped charities to raise money. In 1918 Higgs Dairy wanted to raise money for the Red Cross, so the lids of quart cans were soldered shut and a slot was cut in each for coins to be donated. Posters announcing 'Look out for November 7th' and cans were circulated to all dairies throughout London; the response was astounding. Each district had a centre where the huge collections were taken. The police guarded some premises overnight to protect the money before it was deposited in banks the following day. On 29 November 1918, just after peace was declared, James Higgs handed over a cheque for the staggering amount of £12,747 1s 0d to the Lord Mayor. It represented a remarkable effort by the milkmen and their customers and must have contributed greatly to the care of injured servicemen.

After the First World War the milkman and his customers were seeking to get back to some sort of normality but dramatic changes lay ahead.

Milkman E. C. Gray had his own form of motorised transport when photographed in 1919.

STABLE TIMES: 1920–39

THIS PEACETIME PERIOD was dominated by massive changes in the British dairy industry, which affected the role of the British milkman. The milk prams, now referred to as handcarts, were replaced by the familiar horse and cart milk floats in most parts of the country. The milk bottle had arrived and customers liked this better way of delivering milk. The idea of bottles came originally from the United States, as did many ideas adopted by British milkmen. An issue of *The Leisure Hour* dated 26 September 1874 recorded:

> An enterprising milkman in America furnishes his customers with milk in glass. These bottles are delivered as required, the customer returning the bottle left the day before; and no pitcher, pails, bowls or dishes are necessary.

This was fifty years before the widespread use of bottles in Britain, where the bottle was sealed at the neck with a cardboard disc. There was some resistance, and one employer, Gordon Raymond, wrote to his milkmen, saying that 'the delivery of bottled milk, does away with much of the drudgery of the can rounds, i.e. the can washing, churn and barrow cleaning etc'. The advantage of bottle delivery was that the milkman was relieved of the task of measuring the milk and could deliver more quickly. However, instead of finishing his two daily rounds earlier, the rounds were increased in size. Although there were 30 million milk bottles in circulation by Christmas 1928 there was a shortage, and milkmen were encouraging customers to return empties.

First, however, there needed to be large, efficient processing factories for milk bottling, and vast quantities of milk needed to be moved from farms to processing plants and then to new distribution depots. Glass-lined road tankers were used from 1924, and in December 1927 the first glass-lined railway milk tanks were transported from Calveley in Cheshire and Wootton Bassett in Wiltshire. One single tank replaced three hundred railway churns and the emptying process was quicker and quieter than with churns.

Opposite:
For over forty years the milkman and his horse were welcome visitors to the homes of customers and their children.

Awaiting inspection by Mrs Lloyd George, this early horse-drawn milk float was designed to carry twenty cases of milk in hilly districts.

Ben Davies Junior is seen here with his horse ready to start deliveries. Ben's father was a close friend of the wealthy philanthropist Lord Hailsham, who owned sugar plantations.

Louis Pasteur had visited Aylesbury Dairy in January 1881 and made a comment in the visitors' book about the dairy's determination to fight germs and bacteria. Over a decade earlier he had devised his technique of pasteurisation, which improved the keeping quality of beer and wine. The Danish Pasteuriser came into general use in 1895 and was preferred by the milk industry. Infant mortality rates had been vastly reduced where pasteurisation was implemented.

The first refrigerator was displayed at the Great Exhibition in 1851 and fifteen years later William Lawrence developed the capillary refrigerator.

Pasteurisation and bottling had been carried out on a small scale but companies wanted larger units that required greater mechanisation, and consequently processing factories emerged.

The investment in these factories, bottles, distribution depots and horse-drawn floats for larger rounds was considerable. The Milk Bill and its regulations meant there was a distinct possibility that local authorities would undertake the supply of milk and that milkmen would become council employees. Companies mounted a strong resistance to these proposals, and a pamphlet, written by Ben Davies, tore them to shreds, pointing out the current failures in standards of housing, sanitary conveniences, emptying dustbins and street cleaning undertaken by local authorities. The milkmen remained independent. In 1922 a joke circulated amongst milkmen alleging that a councillor, asked about a new crematorium, said that cream making should not take place in his area.

Many handcarts were altered to hold milk bottles, which in the early days were carried in wooden crates, but the carts were still not big enough for some of the larger rounds. The obsolete brass churns were melted down.

So began the era of the horse-drawn milk float. More milk could be carried, and also groceries and dairy products. The chairman of United Dairies stated in 1928 that, because of the competitive nature of the milk trade, milk prices could not be raised and therefore every effort was to be

Many churn milk prams were converted to carry bottles. These two Higgs milkmen proudly push their handcarts but probably would have preferred a horse-drawn milk float to carry their heavy loads.

Excited South London children crowd around the first bottled-milk float in their area in 1926.

made to build up sales of goods other than milk, making use of a distribution network that was able to reach every house with a regularity and a promptness not equalled even by the Post Office. Competition was so fierce that milkmen offered new customers free milk for one or two weeks, or even tea sets. Milkmen increased their range from dairy items such as cream, eggs, butter and cheese to include jams, tinned fruit, cereals, biscuits and other groceries. Yoghourt (as it was spelt in the 1930s) was also available from 3d to 1s, and milk was 7d a quart for most of the period. These extra goods were stored in the depot in an area known as the servery.

This embarrassed young milkman appeared in a cartoon in *Our Notebook* just as canned deliveries were coming to an end.

DAUGHTER OF HOUSE : " How much is our milk bill ?"
NEW MILKMAN (bashfully) : " Beggin' your pardon, Miss, but my name's Basil."

Milkmen were held in high esteem by their customers. Here twelve boys aged five and six dress as milkmen and sing 'Milk Oh' at the St Barnabas School (Pimlico) concert in 1929.

Processing and bottling were often done elsewhere, so it was no longer necessary for dairies to have a few handcarts operating from a yard behind a dairy shop. Small dairies were merging and larger distribution depots were created. Here there would be a rest room, where the milkman could have a cup of tea before and after his round, and sometimes a meal. It was an ideal place to count the takings and do the books, and for recreations such as darts, cards and table tennis. Most depots had a drying room with heated pipe work, where the milkman's wet clothing could be hung. When a new depot opened, it was the custom to invite the mayor and other local dignitaries, and to make charitable donations to local hospitals.

The practice at the distribution depot was for the milkman to harness his horse and load milk from a refrigerated cold room, which had a bank the

These milkmen excitedly crowd around their hero, Flight Lieutenant Russell of the Redwing Company, at Croydon Aerodrome in November 1931. They wanted to start their own flying club but never realised their ambition.

This was the first UD Magazine, published in 1933. A United Daries milk bottle was placed by a builder in 1936 under the foundation stone of Chelsea Bridge with the message, 'This is one of the UD bottles we use now. Goodness knows what you will be using when this is unearthed.'

same height as his float. Often the milkman himself pulled the float into position, and he loaded it in a way that suited him. He then proceeded to the servery to load his groceries, which he stored in the designated goods compartment. Milk floats varied in design and were purchased from traditional carriage-makers, but some large companies, such as United Dairies at Haycroft Farm, designed and built their own.

In 1926 milkmen working for Curtis & Dumbrill moved to a new depot at Valley Road, Streatham, in south London. It became known as the 'Dairy in the Garden' because of the fifty houses with beautiful gardens built for milkmen and their families, who paid a weekly rent of 15s. In July 1926 the Minister of Health, Neville Chamberlain, visited the dairy, and the Duke and

HUSH! HUSH!

OUR EARLY MORNING MILK IS IN FUTURE TO BE DELIVERED IN CARTS FITTED WITH SILENT TYRES.

Left: Measures were taken to reduce noise levels for early morning deliveries. Even rubber horseshoes were tried, but unsuccessfully. This cartoon appeared in *Our Notebook* in 1933.

Below: Milkmen needed plenty of nerve to navigate through heavy traffic in these small three-wheeled vehicles. This Express milkman is pictured in 1933.

Duchess of York came on 8 December 1927; one of the men, Tom Parr, jokingly offered to give the baby Princess Elizabeth (the future Queen Elizabeth II) riding lessons when she was older.

Milkmen developed a love for their horses, as did the customers and their children, who enjoyed feeding the milkman's horse. The horse soon learned its round and knew where to stop and wait, and when to move on, keeping pace with the appreciative milkman, thus considerably reducing the distance he had to walk. Many horses were Welsh cobs bought as four-year-olds for around £30 and standing fourteen hands. Some worked to a great age and one called Maggie, employed on a round in Wimbledon, was claimed to be thirty-eight, and still working, in 1932. It is said that Sam, a milk pony who developed a kicking habit, was sold to a Bedfordshire farmer, who trained him as a jumper, and that he was sold for nearly £200 to a wealthy American, who shipped him to the United States.

At least one company experimented with rubber horseshoes to quieten the horses' hooves but they were abandoned as they caused lameness.

In 1933 these milkmen and women were holding a pageant showing how deliveries had progressed over the last fifty years. With aviation advancing rapidly, they took a very futuristic view of things to come.

In September 1935 the United Dairies Magazine and Price List, given to milkmen's customers, found it necessary to instruct housewives on how to remove the new foil caps from milk bottles. Women had won the right to vote seven years earlier.

Concerned about the noise of their early morning deliveries, dairies introduced pneumatic tyres to floats from 1932 and, although the horse-drawn float was the main method of delivery, some electric milk floats were appearing by the early 1930s.

In 1926 the same spirit re-emerged that had maintained milk deliveries during the blizzards of Victorian times and the difficulties of the First World War. Although the nation was paralysed by the General Strike, the British housewife and her family could still enjoy their cups of tea thanks to the milkmen. In London, Hyde Park was commandeered and lorries were

United Dairies
employed more
than three
thousand horses.
Their last horse-
drawn float was at
Fulham in 1959.

requisitioned to collect milk from within a 100-mile radius. Milk was then allocated to all milkmen to enable them to serve their customers, and the President of the Board of Trade recorded his thanks on 21 May. Interestingly, Hyde Park had had its own cows in Victorian times, when a milkman named Walker held grazing rights and a lodge-keeper, Mr Gilbert, looked after them.

Weekly credit was a benefit offered by milkmen that was much appreciated by poor families, enabling many to have food on the table during midweek, when money had run out. The milkman was therefore a welcomed caller, held in high esteem. His job was demanding, requiring ability with figures and knowledge of customers' requirements, and only capable, fit young men were normally recruited. They were smartly dressed in uniforms, often with military-style white caps. In 1932 United Dairies introduced a six-day week, giving milkmen a weekly day of rest, and extra staff were recruited to cover rounds in this period of desperate unemployment.

Companies of the period fostered a family atmosphere amongst staff. There were outings for milkmen to seaside resorts and beauty spots. On such occasions, the milkman would start his round extra early, having enlisted the help of customers, who would receive only one delivery after taking extra milk the previous day. There were many social functions, including dances, children's parties and sporting activities. In May 1928 one large dairy company opened a sports pavilion with playing fields at East Lane, Wembley, and so their milkmen could honestly brag that they had played football at Wembley. By the late 1930s, with war again threatening, milkmen enrolled in such activities as first aid and firefighting.

The 1920s and 1930s had seen the British milkman elevated to a position in which everyone respected his demanding job and he was considered by most as a family friend. The dairy industry had gone from selling 'loose' milk to a modern, hygienic industry employing the smartest and most reliable of men. However, milkmen would again be called upon to serve their country on the field of battle.

A MILKMAN DELIVERS — ALFRED CHARLES KNIGHT

Alf Knight was born in 1912 and was fascinated as a boy to see the milkman with his milk pram. When Alf left school he became an apprentice to a baker. At twenty-one he became entitled to a man's wage, which was a signal for an employer to get rid of the man and start another boy apprentice, a common practice in the Depression of the 1930s. He secured a job with Alperton Park Dairies, pushing a handcart from the Wembley Park branch to deliver bottles, which the dairy had introduced a few years beforehand. His was one of eight handcart rounds, along with eleven others at the nearby Ealing Road branch, which had a Servitor electric float. Milk was 3¾d a pint and 7d a quart. Alf knew the value of good service but also that nothing counted as sales until the milk bill was paid, and so he vigorously chased outstanding payments.

There were two attractions for young Alf. One was Elsie, twenty years his senior and manageress of the dairy shop, and the other a brand-new Murphy electric milk float, a rarity in the mid-1930s. Alf was to marry Elsie and was given the new Murphy vehicle, delivered from the manufacturer's works in Maidenhead in 1936. The dairy began in the early 1920s with the owners delivering milk from a churn in the sidecar of a motorcycle. Alf spent the Second World War as a driver in the Army, during which time the Express Dairy took over his old firm.

After the war, he joined another dairy at Sudbury, Middlesex. He kept his electric milk float in top condition: he inspected his float daily for any scratches made by clumsy yard staff when moving the vehicle, and he kept a pot of paint to touch up any damage. After a road accident at the age of sixty-four Alf had a leg amputated and he had to retire. He was fanatical about electric floats and reckoned that with his forty-year experience he had more years of driving electric floats than any other milkman in the country at that time.

Alf Knight.

ELECTRIFYING TIMES: 1940–59

MILKMEN were recruited to serve in the armed forces during the Second World War and many paid the ultimate price. United Dairies had 198 men lost in action and thirty-five members of staff were killed in Britain. Again it was women, boys and older men who kept the doorstep service going.

In the first week of the war black-out regulations made it necessary to reorganise from two deliveries a day to one during the hours of daylight. Households were given a choice of only two milkmen, one independent, and one from the Co-operative.

Despite the bombing, milk was regularly delivered; not infrequently it was left at the front of houses completely demolished, with the knowledge that neighbours would know if the occupants were alive and would take the milk to them. Bombing meant that often milk trains failed to get through and some processing and distribution depots were hit. To release labour, milk rounds were rationalised, and measures were taken to cover the rounds of dairymen whose premises had been blitzed. By the start of 1940 at least 700,000 children and mothers had been evacuated and milk sales fell between 18 and 38 per cent, while in some cities rounds were merged. As a result, many horses became surplus and were sold to the Army. Bombing upset the horses, and milkmen would volunteer to stay all night to keep them calm.

It was not only children who were evacuated, but also substantial numbers of older folk and others with relatives in safer areas. Milk rounds were depleted in the cities but consumption was much higher in those rural districts. Some women took over their husband's rounds when they were called up for duty. In 1940 a lad named Benny Hill, who would later became a world-renowned comedian, started work at Hann's Dairy in Market Street, Eastleigh, Hampshire. No driving licence was needed to drive a horse-drawn float and so, at sixteen, Benny had a round serving Fair Oak.

The Emergency War Budget, introduced by Sir John Simon, included the rationing of petrol, which affected the movement of milk from processing plants to distribution depots, but few milkmen used petrol vehicles for their deliveries. Simon increased sugar duty, leading to higher

Opposite:
The Express Dairy was one of the first milk companies to adopt the new battery electric milk float.

Right: Reassuring words in this newspaper cutting from the Second World War.

Below: Many industrial cities and sea ports were heavily bombed during the Second World War. Here a milkman gallantly carries on with his deliveries amongst the devastation and rubble.

UNITED DAIRIES
WARTIME
SERVICE

THE Pasteurised Bottled Milk Service maintained by the Company is yet another of those outstanding organisations brought into prominence by the War.

Through the difficult times of last autumn and winter, day and night the Service carried on. Many were the tributes paid by a grateful public to the Company's staff for "appearing as usual," as so many put it.

Hard blows have been taken and perhaps harder blows are to come. Whatever they may be, the Nation-wide organisation of United Dairies will be ready.

prices for some products, including sweetened milk. Rationing of foodstuffs was introduced in January 1940 and included dairy produce such as butter and cheese. The National Milk Scheme was introduced, undertaking to deliver priority milk to every household where there were expectant mothers, children or invalids, all of whom were allowed a pint a day. The rest of the population normally received 2 pints a week, although not guaranteed. In March 1945 the weekly ration increased to 2½ pints.

United Dairies sent Christmas parcels to staff serving in the armed forces, and these contained Christmas pudding, chocolate, playing cards, cigarettes and a copy of the staff

magazine, *Our Notebook*. They also made a generous donation towards buying wool for a knitting campaign to send comforts to those serving abroad. After an appeal to return aluminium foil caps from milk bottles for conversion into war material, *The Milk Industry* magazine reported that 80 million had been handed to milkmen in the first few months.

This horse-drawn milk float is driven by Bernard Plumb of Plumb's Dairy, Balsham, near Cambridge. It was used as a poster by the dairy.

"It's a picnic! They let you lie in bed till **6** a.m!"

Was life easier for milkmen in the Army? This cartoon appeared in *Our Notebook* in 1943.

Above: Leyton depot was hit by a bomb on 15 September 1940 but the milk rounds still went out. Bombs also fell on the depot in Gap Road, Wimbledon, tragically killing four members of staff.

Right: A Brush 'Pony' delivered in 1947. Brush Electricals chose the name 'Pony' for their floats to appease the milkmen who had lost their beloved horses, but this only upset the unhappy milkmen even more.

Some milkmen were required to push handcarts long after electric versions were introduced. This 1940s model was owned by Brown & Harrisons. In 1940 Arthur Brown Ltd had merged with Harrison's Model Dairies to create this new company.

With product shortages, rising prices, ration books and registration of customers, and floats hitting kerbs in the blackout, times were difficult for milkmen, but they were determined to ensure the service was kept going.

On VE Day, milkman Harry Sutton had a celebratory cup of tea with his customers. His horse, Snowball, decided to walk the rest of the round on his own and returned to the depot alone, much to the consternation of the depot manager, Mr Eaton, but Harry duly arrived on foot and everyone saw the funny side of the incident.

After the war, many new electric milk floats were provided as dairies invested in new transport. Milkmen were sad to lose their beloved horses, and Alf Avery of Pinner wept openly when his horse, Jumbo, was led away for the last time, but milkmen who had pushed handcarts were less resistant. The Bristol Co-operative Society had three hundred electric vehicles at the outbreak of war, and Home Counties Dairies were operating 150 electrics in 1940, but numbers increased after 1945.

The first battery vehicle to run in Britain was built in 1889 and driven by Frank Crawter of the Chloride Electrical Storage Company. Design progressed and large, heavy electric vehicles were in use during the First World War for refuse collection and for delivery work by breweries and railway companies, but they were too cumbersome for use as milk floats. The first battery electric used on milk rounds is believed to have been a coupé that finished its life in Southport as a milk delivery vehicle in 1923. A three-wheeled vehicle was used to collect bags full of coins at the turnstiles at the Wembley Exhibition Grounds. During the 1920s this was acquired by Alperton Park Dairies and was probably London's first electric float.

The term 'electrification' was used for converting to the cheaper, more modern battery electric that was ideal for short-distance, frequent-stop delivery work. The electric float had a rapid acceleration from a stationary position and experiments in Sheffield during the 1940s showed

The old handcarts have gone and the new electrics have arrived. For some reason they were often referred to as 'walkie-talkies'. Things were changing again for milkmen in the 1940s.

A 1950s Graisley electric handcart. It was easier for the milkman than pushing the old-style handcart. This type of cart was used for rounds near the depot.

that when stopping every 10 yards over a mile the electric was almost three times as fast as the horse, and much faster than a petrol vehicle. Electric floats travelled at around 10 mph and did not consume power while standing idle. Having no internal combustion engine and fewer parts, they were easily maintained, and their life was at least three times that of a petrol vehicle.

Many dairy premises were cramped but thirty electrics could be accommodated in the space previously occupied by ten horses, ten vans, bedding, manure and feedstuff. This allowed some companies to close a nearby branch. The milkman and his electric vehicle could maintain a clean appearance, while the maintenance area did not become as dirty as one for petrol vehicles.

Many milkmen had never had the opportunity to own a motor car, so in post-war Britain they would have had difficulty in mastering the complex controls of a petrol-driven vehicle. However, the electric, with its steering wheel, brake and 'go' pedal, gave them the confidence to drive.

Milkmen did need a driving licence and had to pass a test before being allowed to drive an electric float, although it was permitted to drive smaller milk floats with 'L' plates displayed. The test, taken in a slow-moving electric

Above: This colourful 1956 Morris petrol milk float belonged to Coward Bros of Shaftesbury, Dorset and was used on one of their dairy rounds.

Left: John (Jimmy) James, seen here in 1957, was an excellent salesman and went on to train fellow milkmen in the art of selling. His successful managerial career started when Devonshire Dairies was purchased by United Dairies.

British milkmen deliver to famous people and famous places. Here Bill Lander of Stepney depot is seen delivering near Tower Bridge in early 1957.

float, was easy, and the examiner would soon be satisfied of the driver's capability. Because of a legal loophole, passing the test on an electric qualified the person to drive a car. Milkman Albert Osborne recalled that after he was demobbed he returned to work and, following a minimal amount of training, easily passed his test. He was delighted because he had qualified to drive a car, even though he had no idea how to operate one.

Electrification also led to the introduction of battery-electric propelled handcarts, which first appeared around 1938 and lasted until the 1960s. With their speed at 3 mph, milkmen discovered it was possible to stand on the small ledge behind the arm used for steering, stopping and starting the vehicle, and to ride illegally to the start of the round.

In most depots the milkman was required to unplug his vehicle from the charger, which operated overnight at off-peak rates. The plug needed to be safely hung up to avoid being damaged by other vehicles reversing over it. The loading procedure was the same as with horse vans in that the milkman

A *MILKMAN DELIVERS* — LEONARD WILLIAM EDWARDS

Lenny Edwards loved horses and, at the age of fourteen, he wanted to be a milkman at the nearby Yiewsley depot. It was 1942 and the depot was desperately short of men because of the war, so Lenny became a boy milkman and started on 9 February, with a glowing reference from his headmaster. No driving licence was needed for a horse-drawn milk float but, because he was under age, his father had to act as guarantor in case there were cash irregularities. Milk was rationed, his starting wage was 19s 6d a week and his first horse was aptly named Spitfire.

Len so liked his job that he spent more than fifty years as a milkman until his retirement; remarkably, all that time was spent on the same round. Len was well respected by his customers, for he was always polite, courteous and punctual. He served more than four hundred households and kept time by either speeding up if late or waiting at the end of the road when early. Len was saddened when the depot abandoned horses in the early 1950s. He married Cathy in 1952 and they had two sons. After twenty-five years service he was given a brand-new Wales & Edwards electric milk float, OLN 390E, which was to be his float until he retired. It has been restored and preserved by an enthusiast.

On his retirement there was a grand farewell from the people of Harmondsworth, and Len recalled that some of the children he had served in the war years were now grandparents. He was presented with a statuette of an Edwardian milkman for his exceptional service.

Len Edwards.

loaded milk from the coldroom, where it was checked, and then took on the milk returned from the previous day, normally about fifty bottles, which had been refrigerated overnight and would be delivered at the beginning of the round. After a visit to the servery for the groceries he required, he was then ready to leave the yard.

Milkmen preferred the three-wheel electric float for its greater manoeuvrability in narrow streets and congested areas. The shiny new milk floats attracted many children, who begged the milkman to ride in his float. Milk boys continued to help the milkman and many later became milkmen.

The Express Dairy had one hundred electric milk floats at the outbreak of hostilities. 'Silent Electric Delivery Van' was written on the noticeboard above the float, both as a warning, and to inform passers-by of this strange new type of vehicle. Express could see the way ahead and acquired the firm of T. H. Lewis

Right: Joseph
Ferguson of
Connah's Quay,
Flintshire, was top
milkman in
Deeside in 1958.
He worked for
Hanson's, a
Liverpool-based
dairy. Joe's milk
float does not have
a roof to protect
the milk.

Opposite page:
The town hall at
Faversham, Kent,
provides an early
morning backdrop
as a Mount's Dairy
milkman makes his
deliveries.

Limited, who manufactured electric vehicles and had previously been makers
of milk prams. T. H. Lewis made four-wheel electrics and three-wheel
pedestrian-controlled vehicles that sold for £89 10s with a payload of 400
pounds. Many electric-vehicle manufacturers were located in the Midlands,
where the largest company was Wales & Edwards, based in Shrewsbury.

Peter Mills
is seen here
with his brother,
Michael, and horse,
Jenny. Peter was
one of the last
milkmen to have
a horse-drawn
float with United
Dairies. He
worked from the
Fulham branch and
the photograph
was taken in 1959.

Reg Gartrupp of Job's Dairy driving a petrol vehicle on a countryside round in the 1950s. Milkmen and their rounds were seen throughout Britain at this time.

Right: Many dairy companies had their own house magazine. 'Dink' Hall of Brown & Harrison's is featured on the front page of *Milkmade* as he had achieved earnings of £1,000 a year.

JUNE 1963

They supplied milk companies such as Cambrian United Dairies in Wales, Edinburgh & Dumfriesshire and Hanson & Sons in Liverpool with electric milk floats throughout the 1950s.

Milkmen continued to offer weekly credit and most carried a range of groceries. Deliveries were made seven days a week, the bottles being carried to the doorstep in a hand crate with pots of cream or other tempting products in the middle. The crate was known as the 'Silent Salesman', it being hoped that the housewife, seeing these items, would make an impulse purchase. For thirty years bottles had been carried in wire crates, but in 1955 plastic crates were introduced and at the same time the quart and half-pint milk bottles were phased out, and the 16-ounce pint bottle was universally used.

Starting times varied but the expectation was that the milkman would probably serve around 450 households, doing about six hours of delivery work, and an hour of loading, unloading and book-keeping each day, but on cash-collecting days he might easily work for twelve hours. Most dairies made the milkman responsible for any cash and product shortages and it was therefore important to record accurately all deliveries made and cash received. Customers often did not realise that the milkman had to make up any shortfall from his wages.

Companies continued to merge and late in 1959 many milkmen found themselves working for a new firm – the first to operate milk rounds across England, Scotland and Wales.

After the cows had been milked, the milk was left at the roadside for collection. Here, Dick Stockley collects from Mrs Creswell's farm at Cattistock, Dorset, in a bygone age.

THE NEW ORDER: 1960–79

IN 1959 United Dairies had merged with the Guildford-based firm of Cow & Gate, which operated milk rounds under the Home Counties name, to form a new company, Unigate Dairies, which operated rounds throughout England, Scotland and Wales.

In the early 1960s the milkman reigned supreme in supplying the nation with its daily pint. A few shops sold so-called 'long-life' milk but, apart from dairy shops owned by milk companies, the milkman was the only source of fresh milk.

But shopping habits were changing. The new self-service stores allowed customers to weigh up the merits of various products, and the abolition of retail price maintenance in 1964 enabled shops to become more competitive. The working housewife wanted prepared foods that took less time to cook, and items such as eggs, cheese, milk and cream became less popular. There was less contact between the milkman and his customers, leading to a fall in sales and a weakening of the bond between them. Customers were kept informed of new products and special offers by leaflets delivered by the milkman to the four hundred or so households on his rounds. Milkmen sold Christmas club stamps so that customers could save regularly and spread the financial burden of Christmas. A vast range of Christmas items was available, including a variety of hampers.

Young men of the 'Swinging Sixties' had a different outlook on life. The reality of early morning starts and inclement weather did not appeal to many, nor did the necessity of working seven days a week. Vacant rounds and sickness meant that relief staff were fully occupied, and the drudgery of working seven-day weeks for long periods meant that sales were not maintained. The money earned from two rest-day payments each week was boosting wages, but not through commission. The job had become more difficult in some areas

Since deliveries had begun, it had been more profitable to serve areas of high population. The more doorsteps that a milkman could visit, the more milk he sold. In rural areas it was common for the local dairy to organise

Opposite: Many British milkmen carry a wide range of groceries. In 1971 this Unigate milkman demonstrates his range of products carrying the Farmer's Wife label. 'Farmer's Wife' had been a trademark of the Cow & Gate company, which was a predecessor of Unigate. The milkman is wearing the smock uniform that was replaced in 1976.

This milkman is delivering from an electric handcart in Hoyland, Barnsley, Yorkshire, in 1962. Wire crates are very much in evidence.

A 1960s South Coast Dairies lorry-load of milk on its way from a processing depot to a distribution depot. If the milk arrived late, the milkmen had to wait until it arrived before beginning their rounds. Getting the fresh pint of milk to the doorstep requires a lot of organisation behind the scenes.

rounds on the 'wheel' method. The centre of a small town or village would be divided equally between all rounds, which would radiate like the spokes of a wheel to the outlying districts. Generally, rural rounds were considered more difficult than urban rounds. Terraced houses with no front gardens were the easiest to serve, whereas rural rounds required more walking and travelling.

This milkman is just starting his round – no empty bottles can be seen. All his milk is in wire crates and he is correctly carrying milk in a hand crate.

In the 1970s milkmen were often required to work on Christmas Day. A Christmas card from the time shows two very different characters struggling with their festive deliveries.

Increasing street crime in many urban areas meant that theft and assault, especially on paydays, were a risk. The high-rise blocks of flats that were springing up at this time made the milkman vulnerable to theft of milk and groceries from his vehicle when it was left unattended. Milkmen were generally held responsible for any losses, and many refused to serve blocks

Theft of milk from the doorstep was a problem in some areas in the 1970s. One idea was to provide customers free of charge with a security box, which was sometimes fitted by the milkman for elderly customers.

In the 1970s some inner city areas experienced high levels of theft of milk from the doorstep and cash from the milkman. In some areas mobile shops were introduced for customers to collect milk and to pay, and to protect the milkman.

of flats. The increase in the number of cars meant it was often difficult to find a parking space for the float and this led to additional walking. Inner city areas were now considered more difficult than rural areas, but suburban areas remained profitable, with not too many problems.

Supermarkets wanted customers to shop more often than once a week and focused on milk and bread sales to bring customers through the doors more regularly. By the mid-1970s an increasing volume of fresh milk was being purchased from convenience stores, newsagents and garage forecourts.

Many of the issues that had caused these changes were addressed.

Companies tried harder to recruit a better calibre of milkman, and generally more adequate training was given. Many floats were fitted with robust cash security boxes, with the keys being held at the depot to protect takings. Some floats were fitted out as mobile shops to serve difficult estates, and sliding cage doors were fitted to some vehicles serving blocks of flats.

By 1979 a number of milkmen had introduced a 'milkless day'. The customer was asked to take her deliveries over six days, ensuring that milkmen got one day off each week to spend with their families. Sunday was usually the day off work. Although Sunday working was eventually abandoned by most dairies, it had traditionally been one of the best days for milk sales. For some housewives Sunday was cooking day, and with the whole family at home there would be more tea and coffee drunk. Sales of milk in many cases were 50 per cent higher than on Mondays. One old milkman, Charlie Palmer of Stokes Dairy in Camberley, instructed all new recruits that anyone asking for extra milk or eggs on Sundays was to be sold only 'gold top' or large brown eggs, these being premium-priced items.

In 1963 Britain had an exceptionally severe winter but the milkmen with their indomitable spirit usually got all deliveries completed and ensured that the nation could still have its cup of tea. The British milkman continued to be appreciated by his customers. The Care Code was devised whereby milkmen would look for signs of elderly or infirm customers in trouble. The milkman was often the only regular caller, and therefore in a position to notice if something was wrong. In 1974 Terry Payne, a milkman in Dudley, alerted police to the plight of seventy-one-year-old Dorothy Smith, who had suffered a stroke, and they broke down her door to rescue her.

Although the nation was briefed about the introduction of decimal coinage in February 1971, milkmen did face difficulties, especially with some older customers. With weekly milk bills that never altered, it was easy to convert the total to the new currency. However, the correct method

The Care Code was introduced in the early 1970s. This sticker was displayed on milk-float cabs to remind milkmen and customers of the vital part that milkmen had in looking after the community.

Milkman G. Turner of Portsmouth enlists the help of Shirley Hamilton to ensure that customers got their milk during the blizzards of 1963.

was to convert the price of the individual pint first and then total up. This meant in some cases a small rise in the overall bill, and many failed to see why they were paying more if the price of milk was said not to have risen. One milkman who turned decimalisation to his advantage was Harry Dunstan, who had calculated that about half of his 430 households had a bill ending with half a penny. Harry rounded these bills up but, if challenged, he would grudgingly poke around in the bottom of his cash bag, and the usual response was then not to bother. Harry reckoned that decimalisation netted him just over £1 a week or £50 a year, which was nearly two weeks' wages.

A MILKMAN DELIVERS — JOHN MICHAEL DEADMAN

As a schoolboy, John Deadman would help the milkman whose horse was Nugget in the area near Chelsea Football Club. In 1961, aged fifteen, John got a job with a wage of £4 6s 6d at Fulham Depot as a servery boy. His task was to get the groceries ready for the seventy milkmen who worked there. It was hard work but John enjoyed his job. The depot had recently been electrified, the last horses leaving in 1959. At age seventeen, John was signed up as an under-age milkman. He served many notable customers, including the comedy actor Norman Wisdom, who starred as a milkman in the 1965 film The Early Bird. John proved to be a good salesman and was always well stocked up with cereals, tea and a range of tinned goods under the 'Summer Gold' label, as well as eggs, cheese and the top-selling 'Superity' butter.

John was given an electric handcart but sometimes, instead of walking in front of it, he would perch on the ledge at the front and be propelled along. On more than one occasion a policeman appeared out of the early morning shadows and shouted for him to get down. He served seven hundred customers, and milk was mostly 8d a pint, but a halfpenny cheaper in summer months.

John married Pauline in 1972 and then saw an advertisement in the Evening Standard for milkmen's jobs with houses available with Clifford's Dairies in Bracknell, Berkshire. The couple successfully applied and he joined Clifford's in 1973 at the Yateley branch, where there were eight rounds and a potato-packing plant. John worked hard at improving his sales and was earning around £22 a week, including a good commission element. He gained promotion to supervisor and then moved into management. He will retire after fifty years in the milk industry.

John Deadman joined United Dairies when he was fifteen. He was photographed a few days after starting work.

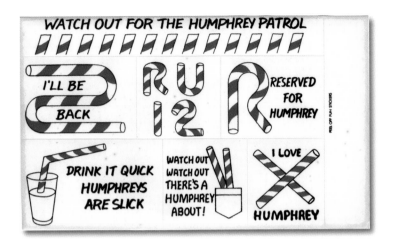

The 'Humphrey' campaign was a memorable television advertising campaign of the 1970s. Stickers were distributed by milkmen to children, and customers could buy Humphrey mugs as well.

In 1971 comedian Benny Hill recorded his hit comedy song 'Ernie' and featured in a number of successful television commercials advertising products for Unigate Dairies. The 'Humphrey' campaign, with the catchphrase 'Watch out, there's a Humphrey about', followed this. It featured an unseen entity stealing milk from a glass and was one of the most memorable series of advertisements in the 1970s.

After many years of customer losses and declining milk and grocery sales, the milkman was fighting back but more changes were necessary to keep the traditional British milkman on the doorstep.

Clifford's dairy commenced trading in 1874. Over a century later, this Clifford's milkman is delivering in Yate, near Bristol.

53

THE MODERN MILKMAN: 1980 TO THE PRESENT

CHANGES IN BUYING HABITS over the previous two decades forced the British milkman to reinvent his role in the 1980s.

The nation was becoming more health-conscious, and the market was right for the promotion of skimmed and semi-skimmed milk, which had become the most popular milk consumed. Semi-skimmed milk was used in a variety of flavoured milks introduced to appeal to children. Fresh orange juice, firstly in cartons and then in glass pint bottles, also became a top seller. Milkmen also recognised the growth in organic products in the 1990s; many began selling organic fruit and vegetables, and soon the organic pint of milk was available to customers. In the early 1980s some milkmen sold wine in boxes. Some milkmen also deliver newspapers and magazines, which is compatible with their early morning delivery routine.

Although milk was of the highest quality, it was in many cases carried on unrefrigerated milk floats. Measures were taken to ensure that milk reached the doorstep in the best possible condition. Many floats were fitted with blinds to keep direct sunlight from the milk. Almost all floats were fitted with insulated cold boxes to ensure the milk was maintained at the same temperature as it was when it left the refrigerated coldroom.

The cost of operating milk rounds continued to rise and measures were necessary to keep rounds profitable. Around 1980 milkmen found themselves delivering the new 'pintie' bottle, weighing only 8 ounces. This replaced the standard bottle, which was much heavier, and a different shape. Some customers doubted that the new bottle contained the full 20 fluid ounces of a pint and a few customers checked this against a retained old-style bottle. Being squatter, these bottles were often referred to as 'dumpy' bottles, but the dairy companies, alarmed that customers might think the term meant disposable, coined the name 'pintie'. Whilst the pint bottle remains popular, many milkmen deliver 4-pint polybottles, popular with heavy milk consumers.

Loss of customers caused many milk rounds to become unprofitable; they were therefore eliminated, and their remaining customers allotted to nearby rounds. The milkman absorbing new customers needed to fit them

Opposite:
Milkman Jimmy
Quinn from the
Unigate depot at
Haycroft Farm.
This modern style
of uniform was
adopted in 1976.

Above: An enterprising milk company had the good idea of making early morning deliveries of milk and newspapers together.

Left: The insulated 'Milk Minder' box appeared in 1990. It protected milk from hot weather and direct sunlight.

Below: An idyllic setting as Fred Tandy delivers on the Stonehills Estate in Tewkesbury, Gloucestershire, in 2003. In 1999 Cotteswold Dairies were the first British dairy to sell organic milk in pint bottles.

into his existing round without any disruption of service and it was not always easy to maintain existing times of delivery. A method of reducing overheads was to close depots and transfer rounds to other depots. In some cases the extra mileage incurred meant the milkman changing from a battery-operated electric float to a motorised vehicle.

In October 1987 a hurricane swept through southern England. At Morden, Surrey, large panes of glass fell from the depot roof but the twenty-two milkmen, including brothers Ron and Ken Beardwell, made sure customers received milk, even though the depot was to close a few days later.

In an effort to reduce costs, companies closed processing plants, and distribution depots needed to be near as possible to the remaining plants to reduce transport costs. This led to further swapping of distribution depots

Mark Cooper of Harlesden with a crate of assorted milk bottles in 1986. Harlesden was the first United Dairies depot to convert from milk can delivery to bottles, sixty years before this photograph was taken.

Terry Gleaves from the Unigate depot at The Manor, Westcott Place, Swindon, pictured in 1990 presenting a customer with a bill from his new electronic round book.

between companies. Customers and milkmen who were transferred to another company were not always happy to have been treated in this way. The strong bond that existed half a century before no longer existed and customer loyalty could not be taken for granted.

Companies continued to merge, and many respected dairies like Clifford's and Job's, both started in Victorian times, ceased to operate. Hindell's, a Yorkshire dairy company started in 1920, had become the large Associated Dairies based in Leeds, but in the 1980s the parent company decided to sell the milkround business and concentrate on its successful Asda supermarkets.

The non-Sunday restricted delivery pattern was pursued and in many cases customers were changed to deliveries on alternate days. The milkman was not off work but did different rounds on different days. While in the early twentieth century the milkman was delivering three times a day, a hundred years later he was delivering three times a week.

One problem that bedevilled the industry before 1980 was the milkman's remuneration package. Milkmen were encouraged to increase sales and companies offered excellent prizes to milkmen. Kenny Hughes won a trip on Concorde. These commission systems were to spur milkmen to sell more milk and groceries and to seek new customers, but the amount of work varied between rounds and the extra commission did not always adequately reward the milkman.

In the early 1980s the franchised structure was introduced, whereby the milkman became self-employed and operated his milk round as a business. He buys his milk and products from the parent milk company, which provides him with a float on a rental basis; the round remains with the company but the milkman enjoys greater rewards. The milkman takes on the responsibility of setting up of bank accounts, insurance and VAT registration, produces annual accounts for tax purposes and adheres to certain standards set out in the franchise agreement. Many milkmen converted to the role of a franchisee and also new entrants were attracted to being franchised milkmen. The parent company usually provides support with advertising material, uniforms, training and advice on running the business.

During the 1990s many milkmen embraced modern technology by adopting the electronic round book. This term was used instead of 'hand-held computer', which alarmed many older milkmen who were convinced that they would not be able to master its complexities. The electronic round book gave an itemised bill and receipt to customers, a more professional method than the handwritten version sometimes used by milkmen. It was capable of precisely calculating customers' bills, and the milkman was relieved of having to add up individual accounts for five hundred or so households. It worked out how much milk and groceries were required for the round, as well as storing information regarding delivery points and directions for relief staff. The information was downloaded daily at the depot and allowed customers to discuss their accounts with depot staff immediately, instead of waiting for the milkman to return to the depot. It helped franchised milkmen in preparing annual balance sheets.

Brian Hanby was the youngest finalist in the 1991 competition to find 'Britain's Best Milkman'. Pictured (left to right) are Barbara Strip (customer), Brian Hanby, Robin Russell and special guest Betty Phelps (the author's wife). The milk float was built by Wales and Edwards in the 1950s, but by the 1990s was used only for promotional purposes.

There were echoes from seventy years earlier of the fears when milk bottles were introduced to replace cans, but, once the milkman was using the electronic round book, he and his customers were happy with the outcome.

Dairy companies further embraced new technology by having their own websites, giving details of their company, the area they serve and their product range. There would be an email address to register variations to requirements, and on rare occasions even to complain. Dairy Crest introduced its 'Milk & More' online service whereby customers can order items before 9 p.m. on the evening before delivery. Extra milk and a vast range of products, including items for gardens and pets, are available. There is no additional charge for the service and it is possible to pay by direct debit

A MILKMAN DELIVERS — NEIL GARNER

When Neil Garner left school he was employed in the aircraft industry but was made redundant in 1994. Married to Sonia, and with a young daughter, Grace, and another daughter, Lily, on the way, he became a milkman with the local St Albans and Enfield Co-operative Society. Neil thoroughly enjoys serving more than five hundred customers in the Colney Heath area. His day starts by getting up just after midnight and cycling to work; he aims to get his first pint on the doorstep by 3 a.m. He recognises how fit the job of a milkman, along with his 90 miles of cycling a week, keeps him. Neil sells nearly 200,000 pints each year, and his non-milk sales total more than £15,000 annually. Top sellers are bottles of orange and other fruit juices, and a number of customers buy bags of garden compost. A large amount of milk is sold in 4-pint polybottles.

Neil was the first milkman in the depot to use a hand-held computer and acknowledges that this has significantly reduced the hours he once spent on balancing round books. Neil and his round transferred from the Co-op to Dairy Farmers of Britain Ltd, and then on to

become one of more than three thousand rounds operated by Dairy Crest, who implemented the 'Milk & More' online scheme. This has been very successful and encourages both new and existing customers to order from the growing range of additional items. Neil's enthusiasm for being a milkman was rewarded in 2007 when he was voted Milkman of the Year by Dairy UK after being nominated by his customers.

Neil Garner is pictured in his Dairy Crest uniform outside the former Co-op depot in an electric milk float once owned by Express Dairy. Many dairy companies merged at the start of the twenty-first century.

or a credit card. The milkman was moving into the twenty-first century.

British milkmen serve three million households and provide a wonderful service in even the most severe weather conditions. They provide a lifeline to many elderly customers and have raised huge amounts for both large and small charities.

Right: The River Severn burst its banks in 1990, but this did not stop milkman Tom Morgan from making his deliveries. A float was originally a raft or flat-bottomed boat, but by Tudor times it also meant a flat-bottomed wagon. It is appropriate to say that Tom is delivering from his float.

Below: Chris Hatch from the now closed depot at Ewelme in Oxfordshire struggles through the snow during 1996. British milkmen deliver whatever the weather.

Mr D. Sheldon of White House Dairy, Knutsford, Cheshire, with part of his fleet of electric and diesel vehicles. His is one of a number of small independent milk companies still operating rounds in Britain.

The milkman has come a long way since the mid-nineteenth century, and the nation's 6,500 milkmen continue to work hard to keep this wonderful British tradition alive, but in a very modern form.

The British dairy industry owns the largest fleet of environmentally friendly commercial battery electric vehicles. Tom Young is seen here in 2007 with the very latest model.

FURTHER READING

Backhouse, G. *Old Trade Handcarts*. Shire, 1982.

Georgano, N. *Electric Vehicles*. Shire, 1996.

Hills, S. M. *Battery Electric Vehicles*. Newnes, 1943.

Hinshelwood, G. *The Old Dairy at Crouch Hill*. Hornsey Historical Society, 1999.

Holton, A. *What Comes With the Milk?* Dairyland Publishing, 1998.

Huins, J. *Choosing a Job. Milkman*. Waylands, 1973.

Ingram, Arthur. *Dairying Bygones*. Shire, 1977.

Jenkins, A. *Drinka Pinta: The Story of Milk and the Industry that Serves it*. National Milk Publishing Council, 1970.

Lewisohn, M. *Funny Peculiar: The True Story of Benny Hill*. MacMillan, 2002. (Gives details of Benny's time as a milkman in 1940, his first record, 'Ernie – the Fastest Milkman in the West', and his television commercials for Unigate Dairies in the 1970s.)

PLACES TO VISIT

Gunnersbury Park Museum, Popes Lane, Acton, W3 8LQ.
Telephone: 020 8992 1612.
Website: www.ealing.gov.uk

National Motor Museum, Beaulieu, Brockenhurst, Hampshire SO42 7ZN.
Telephone: 01590 614650.
Website: www.nationalmotormuseum.org.uk

Rural Life Centre, Reeds Road, Tilford, Farnham, Surrey GU10 2DL.
Telephone: 01252 795571.
Website: www.rurallife.plus.com or www.farnham.gov.uk

Stockwood Discovery Centre, London Road, Luton LU1 4LX.
Telephone: 01582 548600.
Website: www.stockwooddiscoverycentre.com

Weald & Downland Open Air Museum, Singleton, Chichester, West Sussex PO18 0EU.
Telephone: 01243 811363.
Website: www.wealddown.co.uk

INDEX